Great Battles
of
World
War II

Ole Steen Hansen

RAINTREE
STECK-VAUGHN
RSVP® **PUBLISHERS**

A Harcourt Company

Austin   New York
www.steck-vaughn.com

THE WORLD WARS

Published by Raintree Steck-Vaughn Publishers, an imprint of Steck-Vaughn Company

Library of Congress Cataloging-in-Publication Data
Hansen, Ole Steen.
Great battles of World War II / Ole Steen Hansen.
    p.   cm.—(The World Wars)
    Includes bibliographical references and index.
    ISBN 0-7398-2757-X
    1. World War, 1939–1945—Campaigns—Juvenile literature.
    2. Battles—Juvenile literature. [1. World War, 1939–1945—
    Campaigns. 2. Battles.] I. Title. II. Series.

    D743 .H328 2001
    940.54'2—dc21   00-062836

Printed in Italy. Bound in the United States.
1 2 3 4 5 6 7 8 9 0 05 04 03 02 01

Picture acknowledgments
AKG 15, 33, 36, 37, 38, 46, 48, 56; Camera Press cover (main); HWPL 10, 12 (bottom), 17, 43, 49 cover (inset top); Peter Newark's Military Pictures 5, 6, 8, 9, 11, 12 (top), 13, 18, 19, 20, 22–3, 25 (top), 28, 29, 32, 40, 41, 44, 47, 50, 51, 57 cover (inset middle); Novosti 35; Popperfoto 7, 21, 25 (bottom), 30, 31, 39, 45, 52, 53, 54, 58; Topham 16, 26.
Main cover photograph: the war in the Pacific. Stars and Stripes raised on top of Mount Saribachi on Iwo Jima, by a Regimental Combat team of the U.S. 5th Marines, February 23, 1945. Insets: (top) the badge of the British XIV divsion, who fought in Burma; (lower) a German regiment. Map artwork by Peter Bull.

Introduction

When Japan attacked China in 1937 and Germany later attacked Poland in 1939, the world was led into the greatest conflict it had ever seen. World War II was fought on land, at sea, and in the air over large parts of the world. Millions lost their lives in battles that eventually led to the defeat of the nations that had started the conflict. No battle was decisive in itself. The war was fought by the most powerful industrialized nations of the world, and all fought desperately to win. All had courageous soldiers, and good and bad generals. World War II was a war of attrition. The nations with the greatest resources of manpower, weapons, and supplies eventually prevailed—it could not be won by single masterstrokes of inspired generalship.

Yet some battles stand out as important turning points. In these battles, the attackers were stopped for the first time or suffered such grievous losses that they retreated. This book examines the battles that marked the changes of fortunes in World War II.

A map showing the great battles of World War II, fought in Europe and North Africa, between 1939–45.

The Battle of Britain

At daybreak on September 15, 1940, southern England was covered in mist. After the mist had cleared, it would become a fine day—which meant that attacks by German aircraft could be expected. Since July, the *Luftwaffe*, the German air force, had attacked channel shipping, British airfields, and aircraft factories. It had then switched its main attention to London, and in the long weeks that followed battles were fought in the sky. These air battles became known as the Battle of Britain. The aim of the *Luftwaffe* was to destroy the Royal Air Force (RAF) and pave the way for Operation Sea lion— the proposed German invasion of England by sea. Nazi Germany had already conquered Poland, Norway, Denmark, the Low Countries, and France. In the latter part of 1940, Great Britain was the only nation still trying to stop the advancing Germans.

A pilot of 85 Squadron RAF Fighter Command steps down from his Hurricane. During the Battle of Britain, losses from the squadron were heavy: 15 aircraft needed to be replaced to keep the squadron up to its usual strength of 12. However, the squadron was credited with shooting down 29 German aircraft.

A painting showing British Spitfires fighting with the Luftwaffe, the German air force, in the skies over London. Together with the Hurricane, the Spitfire was the plane that kept the Luftwaffe at bay in 1940.

By late morning, radar stations reported German aircraft joining up in large formations over France. Usually, small groups of British fighters had to attack large German formations of aircraft. But for once, enough warning had been given to the defending fighters to allow plenty of squadrons to take off from their airfields. Thanks to the very efficient system of radar, the British fighters were ready for the German onslaught. The first Spitfire squadrons attacked the Germans over Kent, and later other squadrons fought the Germans all the way to London and finally over the city itself.

Bombs fell in many London areas, including Westminster, Lambeth, Crystal Palace, and Clapham but the bombing was scattered and inconclusive. Dogfights raged as the German fighters tried to protect the slower and less maneuverable bombers from British attacks. One British pilot flew so close while firing his guns at a German bomber that his own Hurricane went out of control when the German aircraft exploded in front of him. Miraculously, both the British and German airmen survived the encounter, although the British pilot landed in a garbage can in Chelsea. Parachutes didn't give airmen much control over where they landed!

Later in the afternoon, more German attacks were made by three waves of aircraft crossing the coast at five-minute intervals. Refueled and rearmed, the British fighters once again took them on with the same devastating results for the *Luftwaffe*. Their claims that

185 Germans had been shot down were highly exaggerated as the figure was only 60, but the losses were still a severe setback to the Germans. The RAF lost 26 fighters, from which 13 pilots managed to escape by parachute. Many German bombers returned home damaged, with dead or wounded airmen on board. The German intelligence and media had given the impression that the RAF was at breaking point but the massed formations of British fighters proved otherwise. The huge air battles over London on September 15 were not decisive in themselves but they made Hitler postpone Operation Sea lion "until further notice." The plan was never carried out.

The accumulated weeks of fighting sapped the strength of both the RAF and the *Luftwaffe*. However the bombing continued through the autumn and winter, when the Germans attacked British cities under cover of darkness. But as the daylight air battles faded out in October, it became clear that, for the first time, Hitler's forces had not won a battle. In order to defeat Great Britain, Germany needed air superiority over the British Isles, but this had been denied to them by RAF Fighter Command. In the aftermath of the battle, neither the British Army nor the RAF was capable of launching any serious attacks on Germany. The Battle of Britain was lost by Germany more than actually won by an exhausted Great Britain.

The Battle of Britain inspired young Americans to volunteer for service with the RAF. Here, men of the first "eagle" squadron run to their Hurricanes. The squadron was later transferred to the U.S. Army Air Force (USAAF) when it entered the war.

In the years ahead, the air war against Germany would be launched from Great Britain. Great Britain would also be the base where the Allied forces would be built up for the attack on the beaches on D-Day in 1944. All this was nothing but a dream in 1940. Nonetheless, the Battle of Britain was the first in a series of great battles that would change the course of the war—the first tiny flicker of light at the end of the very long tunnel that led to the defeat of Nazi Germany.

Although daytime battles faded out in October 1940, German bombers continued to attack British cities into 1941. Here, in London, civilians have been bombed out of their homes.

The few

"Never in the field of human conflict was so much owed by so many to so few." With these words, Winston Churchill summed up the gratitude felt toward the young men flying the Spitfires and Hurricanes defending Great Britain. Altogether, 3,000 fighter pilots flew with the RAF at one time or another during the battle. Although 80 percent of these were from the UK, "the few" represented a broad cross-section of nations fighting—or occupied, by Germany. For example, 147 were Poles, 101 New Zealanders, 94 Canadians, 87 Czechs, 29 Belgians, 22 Australians, ten Irish, seven Americans, and there was one Palestinian. Of the ten fighter pilots who shot down 14 or more German aircraft during the battle, two were from New Zealand, one was from Australia, one was from Czechoslovakia, and one was from Poland.

El Alamein

When Great Britain declared war on Germany in 1939, few would have guessed that for four long years there would be little fighting on land in western Europe. But from June 1940 to June 1944, the British, German, and Italian armies fought each other only in the Mediterranean area of western Europe. In fact, the first large-scale battle in which the Allied forces won a decisive victory was fought in Egypt.

Italians defeated

Italy declared war on Britain on June 10, 1940—just before the German army forced the surrender of France. Both the British and Italians had troops in North Africa and they began fighting. For the Italians, the defeat of the British army in the desert would mean that the road to the Suez Canal and the oil in the Middle East would be open. This was significant because both of these were of extreme importance to the British.

British forces—including troops from Australia, India, and New Zealand—were under the command of General Archibald Percival Wavell. Initially, they had great success, and by the end of the first months of 1941 they had defeated the Italians. They captured 130,000 Italian soldiers and 400 tanks, with the loss of 500 British soldiers. Unfortunately, due to his limited resources, Wavell could not completely secure the north coast of Africa. In the spring of 1941, British troops were sent to help Greece, which had come under German attack. The combined British/Greek forces were not able to stop the Germans. In Syria and Iraq (an essential supplier of oil to Great Britain), pro-German governments took over. Wavell had to send troops to make sure these areas remained pro-British.

A motorcycle and a machine gun are the spearhead of a German panzer (tank) division in the desert campaign. The desert sand caused heavy wear on vehicles and engines.

The Afrika Korps arrives

These moves gave the Germans time to send support to Africa. The Afrika Korps, under the command of Field Marshal Erwin Rommel completely changed the situation in the desert. Rommel was a master of using his mobile forces in the open spaces of the desert.

Time and again he would outflank the British forces and their allies by driving south at first and then around them. Hard battles were fought, and Tobruk, in Libya was held for many months. However, by 1942 the Afrika Korps had pressed the British and their allies all the way back to Egypt.

Tobruk was defended by the British, Australians, New Zealanders, South Africans, and Polish troops. After a siege in 1941, it eventually fell to Rommel's forces in 1942 on their drive toward Egypt. Here, the first Germans to enter the town are seen in the main square.

However, as the Germans advanced, it became difficult to dispatch water, fuel, weapons, and other supplies to their troops. These had to be sent by boat from Italy and then transported along the coast road. Allied air and naval strikes—some of which came from the British island of Malta—greatly reduced the supplies that reached the Afrika Korps. Sometimes, the soldiers had only just enough water for drinking and filling up the radiators of their vehicles. Washing was out of the question, although a shower would have been a welcome luxury in the heat and dust. Many of the Afrika Korps suffered from the poor diet, which consisted mainly of canned sardines and sausages.

In 1942, when the Afrika Korps reached the small train stop of El Alamein in Egypt, they were exhausted. The British and their allied forces were also exhausted, but here they managed to contain the advance of the enemy. At El Alamein there could be no outflanking by the Afrika Korps. South of the battlefield lay the impassable salt marshes known as the Qattara Depression. To the north was the sea. The opposing armies had no alternative but to fight head-on. The Afrika Korps could not break through the British lines. The Germans and their allies then fortified their positions at El Alamein. They created a strong system of minefields, anti-tank guns, and other weapons extending to a depth of 5 miles (8 km).

A British Crusader tank moves up to the front line at El Alamein along dust tracks.

The British attack

The British forces in the desert, known as the Eighth Army, were now under the command of General Bernard Law Montgomery. Although not necessarily more fit than the Africa Korps, his men underwent hard training. Montgomery's army was also superior in tanks and artillery. Good generalship and great courage from the soldiers were needed to push back the enemy. On October 23, the Eighth Army attacked over a broad front to disguise where the really heavy blows would hit. New Zealanders and Australians played key roles in the attack alongside the British, but soldiers from France, Czechoslovakia, and Greece also took part. Army doctrine suggested that tanks should pave the way for infantry. Montgomery let the infantry pave the way for the tanks, through the minefields.

British gun blast a way through Axis defences in North Africa

BACK THEM UP!

Above: A British poster featuring the desert war

Fighting in the desert in November 1942. Eighth Army troops with fixed bayonets charge at their enemies. The battle for El Alamein turned into eleven days and nights of close-combat fighting.

Erwin Rommel (1891–1944)

During World War I, Rommel had proved himself to be a courageous soldier and had gained the highest distinction. In May 1940, Rommel was one of the German panzer commanders who swept away all opposition in France. Rommel is best remembered for his African campaign where he became known as the "Desert Fox." He was an advocate of fast, sometimes risky, moves that secured him victory in many battles. In the end, lack of supplies and the stronger Allied forces defeated the Afrika Korps. In 1944, Rommel was wounded in an air attack while commanding the German army in Normandy. He no longer believed German victory was possible and was suspected of having taken part in a plot against Hitler. He was given the choice of a trial for high treason or suicide. He chose the latter. His family was not prosecuted—a sign that, after all, Nazi Germany held its hero of the desert war in high respect.

On October 25, a British tank commander claimed that the offensive had become bogged down and wanted to withdraw. Montgomery discovered "to his horror," that the commander was some 10 miles (16 km) behind his leading tanks. He was told to move forward immediately, continue the attack, and "lead his division from in front and not from behind." The attack had to be pushed on in spite of the Germans resisting furiously. Montgomery carefully husbanded his forces, however, pushing forward slowly against fierce resistance.

Field Marshal Erwin Rommel, the shrewd Desert Fox—during the North African campaign 1941–42. At the end of 1943, Rommel was transferred to northern France to defend against the Allied invasion.

On October 27, the Afrika Korps counterattacked but suffered heavily. The following day, they carried out reconnaissance to find the British anti-tank guns and any weak spot in the lines. But as they tried to assemble the tanks for a new attack, the RAF dropped more than 80 tons of bombs on them in two hours. On November 2, British tanks smashed Rommel's last counterattack. Soon the Afrika Korps started retreating, and their vehicles were strafed and bombed

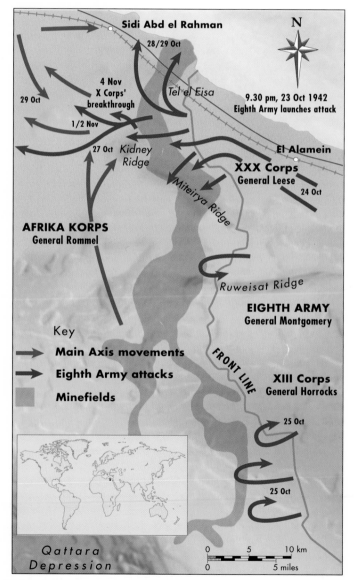

Sidi Abd el Rahman

N

28/29 Oct

4 Nov
X Corps'
breakthrough

Tel el Eisa

29 Oct

9.30 pm, 23 Oct 1942
Eighth Army launches attack

1/2 Nov

27 Oct Kidney
Ridge

El Alamein

XXX Corps
General Leese

Miteirya Ridge

24 Oct

AFRIKA KORPS
General Rommel

Ruweisat Ridge

EIGHTH ARMY
General Montgomery

Key

Main Axis movements

Eighth Army attacks

Minefields

FRONT LINE

XIII Corps
General Horrocks

25 Oct

25 Oct

Qattara
Depression

0   5   10 km
0   5 miles

A map showing the battle at El Alamein. Montgomery fought the battle with more men, tanks, guns, and planes than Rommel. The deep minefield laid by Rommel's troops failed to keep the Allied forces back.

as they made their way westward. It had taken eleven days to advance through the enemy's defenses. The speed of less than one kilometer per day shows the severity of the fighting. Churchill later wrote: "It may almost be said, before Alamein we never had a victory. After Alamein we never had a defeat." Although the small word "almost" covers some serious setbacks, El Alamein was the major turning point in the Mediterranean war.

Below: Montgomery surveys the scene at El Alamein from his tank. The victory at El Alamein and his subsequent pursuit of Rommel was the last victory of the war achieved without the help of the Americans. From then on, the Americans were involved in the fighting.

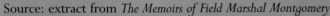

Bernard Law Montgomery (1887–1976)

General Montgomery had the gift of inspiring the men serving under him. Just before the battle of El Alamein he issued a personal message to all officers and men:

"We are ready now. The battle which is now about to begin will be one of the decisive battles in history. It will be the turning point of the war. The eyes of the whole world will be on us, watching anxiously which way the battle will swing. We can give them their answer at once, 'It will swing our way'... The sooner we win this battle... the sooner we shall all get back to our families ... Therefore, let every officer and man enter the battle with a stout heart, and with the determination to do his duty so long as he has breath in his body. AND LET NO MAN SURRENDER SO LONG AS HE IS UNWOUNDED AND CAN FIGHT."

Source: extract from *The Memoirs of Field Marshal Montgomery*

Torch and Italy

The Afrika Korps was soon confronted with a new problem. On November 8, 1942, U.S. and British forces landed in French North Africa for Operation Torch. The U.S. forces took part in their first battles with the Germans. There were hard lessons for them to learn from the experienced Afrika Korps. But it was only a matter of time before the German and Italian forces in Africa surrendered. Talented generalship and courage could take an army only part of the way. Ultimate success depended on the numbers of men, tanks, guns, trucks, and aircraft. Also crucial were supplies of food, ammunition, medical services, and equipment. Unwisely, the Germans tried to reinforce their Afrika Korps using transport aircraft. From El Alamein to their surrender in Africa in May 1943, the Germans lost 2,422 aircraft in the Mediterranean. This was significant because it left the flying schools needed to train new pilots seriously short of instructors.

American troops land at Mers-el-Kabir in the Oran area of the western desert to attack the Afrika Korps from the west.

The battles in North Africa were small compared to the battles on the Eastern front. But they helped to put more pressure on Germany. The long campaign up through Italy also added pressure and lasted through the rest of the war. Churchill liked the idea of attacking through "the soft underbelly of Europe." But there was nothing soft about fighting in the mountains of Italy. The Allied soldiers struggled, as the terrain favored the defense. The wisdom of fighting this campaign has since been questioned. But in 1943, an invasion of France was still not possible for the Western Allies. The campaign in Italy was a way of helping the Russians, who were fighting on the Eastern front, while at the same time preparing for the D-Day attack, which would come in June 1944.

Turning points: the Pacific

While nations in western Europe became involved in the war against Germany, Japan began to expand into the colonies of European powers in Southeast Asia. The United States disapproved of Japanese expansion and relations between the United States and Japan deteriorated. The Japanese bombing of Pearl Harbor on Oahu Island, Hawaii, in 1941 was a surprise attack on the operating base of the U.S. Pacific fleet. The result was devastating: 18 U.S. ships were hit and more than 200 aircraft destroyed or damaged, and the lives of 2,400 Americans were lost. Japan's tactics were to cripple U.S. naval power in the Pacific. But the attack also resulted in the immediate entry of the United States. into the war: "December 7, 1941," said President Franklin D. Roosevelt, "is a date which will live in infamy."

Japan's devastating opening blow against the U.S. Pacific fleet from six aircraft carriers caught the Americans completely by surprise at Pearl Harbor.

The United States fought the war on two fronts. They wanted to secure victory in Europe over Germany and in the Pacific against Japan. War in the Pacific had to be fought over the extreme distances of the world's largest ocean.

After Pearl Harbor, Japan quickly expanded its territory. The European colonial powers and the U.S. forces seriously underestimated the strength of the Japanese. Earlier secret reports on the Japanese Zero fighter's superior range, speed, and maneuverability had been rejected as impossible nonsense. No one could build a fighter *that* good. The feeling of Western superiority changed almost overnight into a myth of Japanese invincibility. It seemed as if nobody could stop the Japanese. Singapore fell, Burma fell, Darwin in Australia was bombed, and American forces were thrown out of the Philippines. For those who were captured by the Japanese, many suffered brutal treatment from their captors and many prisoners died.

Japanese Zero fighters prepare to take off from an aircraft carrier—as painted by a Japanese artist. The excellent Zero played a key role in the Japan's military conquests, although better American fighters were developed during the war.

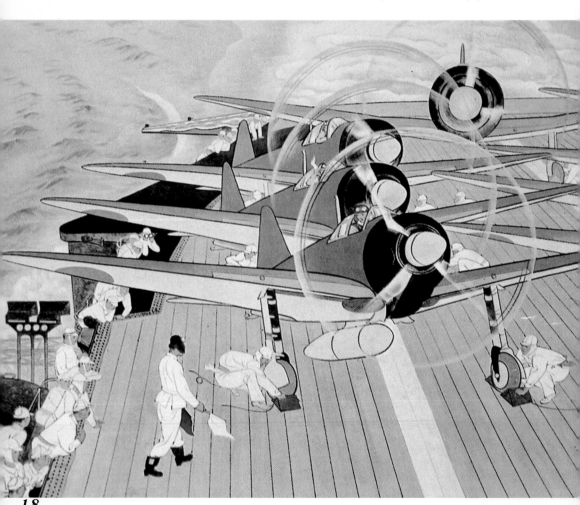

Japan realized it had to fight a short, hard-hitting campaign before the United States could build up superior forces using its enormous industrial capacity. In the summer of 1942, Japan wanted to establish an outer ring of defense to protect its newly won empire. To the south, it wanted to cut the lines of communications between Australia and the United States—and this led to the battles in the Coral Sea and at Guadalcanal in the Solomon Islands. In the central Pacific, Japan hoped to destroy what was left of the American Pacific fleet. This led to the Battle of Midway.

Japanese troops pull down the Stars and Stripes after the surrender of the U.S. forces at Corregidor in the Philippines, May 6, 1942.

Coral Sea

The battle of the Coral Sea was the first in world history in which the opposing navies had no sight of each other. All the fighting took place between aircraft flying from aircraft carriers. In early May 1942, Japanese ships— among them three aircraft carriers— entered the Coral Sea between the Solomon Islands and northeast Australia. The U.S. navy had two of its four Pacific carriers—the *Lexington* and *Yorktown*—in the Coral Sea, together with a number of smaller ships. During the following days, one Japanese carrier was sunk and one badly damaged. The Japanese pulled back. On the U.S. side, both the *Yorktown* and *Lexington* were damaged by Japanese torpedoes. Aircraft carriers were extremely vulnerable ships. Their size made them easier to hit than smaller ships. They carried large amounts of fuel and ammunition for their aircraft. The fate of the *Lexington* was sealed by its own cargo. Fires resulting from broken fuel pipes soon made it necessary to abandon the ship, and many on board were helped to safety. The order was

Battle of the Coral Sea: the Japanese aircraft carrier Shoho *is sunk by American planes from the aircraft carriers* Lexington *and* Yorktown.

Japanese writer Masataka Okumiya described how the failure to finish off the U.S. aircraft carrier *Yorktown* after the Coral Sea battle was a grave mistake:

"None of our surviving officers of the Coral Sea battle could have foreseen the terrible strategic implications of their colossal blunder. The crippled Yorktown *was permitted to escape when perhaps a single torpedo or only a few bombs could have ensured that vessel's destruction. A month later, that same ship which we had permitted to survive became one of the strongest factors contributing to our navy's shattering defeat in the Battle of Midway."*

Source: Martin Caidin: *The Zero Fighter*

given by the Americans to sink the doomed *Lexington* with U.S. torpedoes. The Japanese claimed the battle to be a great victory, since 25 percent of the U.S. carrier strength had been sunk. But, more rightfully, the battle was also regarded to be a victory by the Americans. For the first time, Japan was stopped, and the trained airmen lost were far more difficult to replace for the Japanese.

After first being hit by Japanese bombs, the Lexington *seemed to be in no danger of sinking. Then a spark from a generator ignited vapor from broken fuel lines causing fires and an explosion. The Americans had no choice but to sink their aircraft carrier.*

Midway

Midway is a small island between Japan and Hawaii. The Japanese commanders wanted to attack it, expecting that the U.S. Navy would try to defend it. In doing so, the U.S. Navy could then be destroyed by the vastly superior Japanese fleet. In June 1942, more than 150 Japanese warships—including four aircraft carriers, nine battleships, and six troop ships transporting 2,500 soldiers—steamed toward Midway. Against them the U.S. Navy could only muster 76 ships, with no battleships and only three carriers—the *Hornet, Enterprise,* and *Yorktown,* the last one hastily repaired after the damage suffered in the Coral Sea. However, the Americans did possess an invaluable asset. American intelligence knew the Japanese codes—they knew an attack was coming but they did not know when it would fall. The Japanese attacked the Aleutian Islands in the northern Pacific on June 3. This was meant to divert part of the U.S. Navy, but knowing of the Japanese intentions, the main body of the U.S. Pacific fleet stayed to defend Midway.

Land-based planes from Midway attacked Japanese ships on June 4 but caused little damage. Japanese Zero fighters sent from the carriers successfully shot down many American planes. The U.S. Buffalo fighters fared worse, as none made it back to Midway. Meanwhile, bombers from the Japanese carriers attacked Midway, causing great damage to the airfield. By the early morning, the Japanese planes were landing back on the carriers, having clearly done very well. Their decks were soon scenes of hectic activity. Planes were refueled and armed for a second strike.

Just then, the Japanese ships were attacked by Devastator torpedo bombers from the U.S. carriers. Groups of Zeros quickly took off to deal with these slow aircraft. The first wave of 15 Devastators from the *Hornet* were quickly annihilated—many before they had a chance to drop their torpedoes. Soon, 14 Devastators from the *Enterprise* met the same fate, although four managed to escape the fighters and anti-aircraft guns. Shortly afterward, 12 Devastators from the *Yorktown*

Battle of Midway: a painting of a Grumman TBF Avenger torpedo bomber attacking a Japanese vessel. This battle was the Avenger's baptism of fire. It did not perform very well, since nearly all six attacking Avengers were lost. Later, however, the bomber played an important role in many Pacific battles.

came skimming in low over the water protected by Wildcat fighters that were diving, climbing, and turning desperately in an attempt to fight off the Zeros. A few Zeros went down but once again all the American torpedo planes were shot out of the sky before they inflicted any damage. The American torpedo pilots had paid a terrible price, but it had not been in vain.

Dive-bombers

The men on the Japanese ships had followed the noisy battle low down over the waves, and now the Zeros again prepared to land on the carriers. As this happened, Dauntless dive-bombers from the *Enterprise* and *Yorktown* came screaming down. With difficulty, they had found the Japanese ships, although the dive-bombers from the *Hornet* never did. But the delay turned out to be to their benefit, as all Japanese attention had been focused on the unlucky low-flying Devastators. Flying high, the approach of the 54 dive-bombers had not been noticed. Now it was. Within six minutes three Japanese carriers were hit by a total of just nine bombs—most bombs missed their targets. The bombs didn't destroy the ships, but the resulting conflagration of burning fuel and exploding ammunition in the hulls did. If ever nine bombs had a profound effect on world history, these ones had.

Later in the day, bombers from the last surviving Japanese carrier managed to damage the *Yorktown*. But U.S. dive-bombers soon sank this Japanese carrier, too. More fighting would take place in the sea around Midway, but after the first day the issue was decided. Japan had lost its four most important ships, and hundreds of irreplaceable mechanics and pilots went down with them. These four carriers had all taken part in the attack on Pearl Harbor. In spite of still having far more ships, the Japanese fleet turned around. Without air cover, the other ships could not survive. Amazingly, a few days short of six months after Pearl Harbor, the Japanese had lost their vital superiority in aircraft carriers.

Aircraft carriers

Before the war, senior navy officers of all nations imagined that the battleship would be the dominant vessel in a war at sea. Naval commanders quickly realized that aircraft carriers were far more important. The battles of the Coral Sea and Midway were decided by aircraft flying from carriers. After the battles, both the United States and Japan worked hard to supply their navies with more carriers. Japan only managed to build a few. This was not the case in the United States, where no less than 131 carriers were being constructed or on order within a month of Midway. When U.S. forces attacked the island of Okinawa in 1945, they were supported by more than 1,000 aircraft from 47 aircraft carriers.

Guadalcanal

Guadalcanal is a rugged, sparsely populated island in the Solomons. Its jungles were—in the words of a veteran—"alive with slithering, crawling, scuttling things; with giant lizards that barked like dogs, with huge red furry spiders, with centipedes and leeches and scorpions, with rats and bats...and myriads of sucking, biting, burrowing insects, armies of fiery white ants, swarms upon swarms of filthy black flies and clouds of malaria-bearing mosquitoes."

In 1942, the Japanese were preparing to build an airfield at Guadalcanal, which would help attack communications between the United States and Australia. The Americans decided to ruin these plans. U.S. Marines landed on

Battle for Guadalcanal—a U.S. Marine, his face smeared with protective cream, operates a flame-thrower during the bitter fighting for the island.

Guadalcanal on August 7, 1942 their first amphibious assault since 1898, and their first offensive operation against Japanese-held territory. Control of the area around the airfield was quickly established, but soon the Japanese sent reinforcements to the island. Over the coming months, both sides faced the difficulty of supplying men on a battlefront thousands of miles from their home bases. Food, ammunitions, medical supplies, and reinforcements had to be shipped to Guadalcanal. Both sides did their best to sink the enemy ships, and hard air and sea battles were fought. The Americans discovered just how good the Japanese sailors were at night-fighting.

Members of the U.S. forces wounded on New Georgia Island. This was one of several Pacific islands that the U.S. forces aimed to take as they fought their way toward Japan after the victory at Guadalcanal.

25

In the end, the American forces prevailed. If the Americans had at first underestimated the Japanese, then the Japanese also had seriously underestimated the fighting qualities of the American soldiers. Much fighting took place on ridges around the all-important American-held airfield. It was hand-to-hand combat— sometimes at night—with confusing nerve-racking explosions, shadows, shouts, and screams everywhere. Troops lived for months in their jungle foxholes. The apparently never-ending ordeal in the jungle made them feel lonely, isolated and cut off from the world. Survivors lost as much as 51 lb (23 kg) of their body weight because of the terrible living conditions.

The pilots flying to defend the American positions made a vital contribution to the battle, but they too suffered from the strain of it. John A. DeChant, a marine pilot, wrote how "the airmen felt very unlike the giant killers that the headlines called them. They were sick. Dysentery racked their bowels and stomachs. Malaria shivered and burned them. The tasteless food seemed only to nurture the gnawing of the hunger rat in the bellies. And sleep—sleep was a dream…but there was no break. The work and weariness went on for those who flew."

Finally, the U.S. forces managed to expel the Japanese. On February 9, 1943, the battle was over. A total of 1,592 Americans died on Guadalcanal, while 4,183 were wounded. More than 5,000 were stricken with malaria. At sea, U.S. losses equaled this and may have been greater. Japanese losses were much higher— probably as many as 50,000 died on Guadalcanal, in the air or at sea around the island.

Until 1943, the war in the Pacific had been a question of desperately trying to slow down Japanese progress. Japan was now on the defensive. There would be many more grueling battles on the islands across the vast Pacific Ocean, but the U.S. forces had turned the tide of the Pacific war.

The United States kept fighting in the Pacific until the end of the war. The battle at Okinawa, which ended in victory for the United States, in June 1945, was the most bitter battle of the Pacific war, with huge losses on both sides.

Robert Leckie, a decorated marine machine-gunner who fought at Guadalcanal, has described how the exhausted marines sailed away once the battle was over:

"So they went out to their ships, with 'hell' etched on their faces and evident in their sticks of bones and ragged dungarees. They went out so weak that they could not climb the cargo nets and the sailors, weeping openly, had to haul them aboard or fish them from the bay into which they had dropped. They lay on the grimy decks of these blessed ships, gasping, but happy. And then they heard the anchor chains clanking slowly up the hawse pipes and they struggled to their feet for a last look at Guadalcanal."

Source: R. Leckie: *Challenge for the Pacific*

After Pearl Harbor, the Japanese forces advanced rapidly across Southeast Asia. This map shows the key battles of 1941–42 and the extent of Japan's empire in 1942.

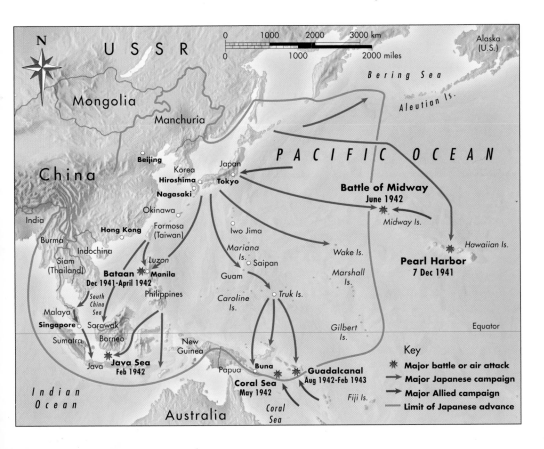

The Eastern front

The invasion of Russia by the Germans in 1941, called Operation Barbarossa, took the Russians completely by surprise. At first, the Germans made startling progress—moving toward Leningrad in the north via the Baltic states, the center via east of Smolensk, and to the south toward the Ukraine and Kiev. In the first 18 days of their campaign they advanced 400 miles (640 km), taking thousands of prisoners, tanks, and guns. They captured Minsk, Smolensk, and then Kiev. Victory for the Germans seemed imminent as they captured a million Soviet prisoners in the first month.

The war on the Eastern front was completely different from the war fought elsewhere in Europe. It was a struggle between two of the most reckless dictatorships the world had ever seen. It became a war of almost incomprehensible hardship and suffering for the soldiers and civilians involved. The German attackers, in accordance with Nazi ideology, considered the local population to be *Untermenschen*—subhumans—and treated them accordingly. The Russians would become slaves—but only those that the German "master race" decided were worthwhile keeping alive.

German tanks advance into the endless steppes of Russia. German propaganda liked to show the mobile tank forces, but most of the German army was in fact moved by horses or by men marching.

A burning village in Russia. The Nazi educational system had taught the German youth to have no respect for the population of Russia. Civilians suffered immensely under German occupation.

War crimes

The list of German war crimes in Russia is depressingly long, and space allows only a few to be mentioned here. Prisoners of war were starved to death or left out in the open to freeze to death in sub-zero temperatures after their overcoats had been taken away from them. The great majority of Russian prisoners of war died in German captivity. People were randomly kidnapped to work as slaves in Germany, many hundreds of villages were burned down, and in some cases, the entire population of villages were shot. *Einsatzgruppen*—special squads—killed hundreds of thousands, mostly Jews, behind the front. Not all Germans in Russia committed crimes, and not all agreed with the German policy. But many did and, on the Eastern front, both sides fought with unparalleled ferocity. Later in the war, the advancing Red Army committed crimes against the civilian population of Germany, but never in the same organized way that the Germans had in Russia.

Born to die

The German and Russian leadership both expected their soldiers to fight under trying circumstances and with little prospect of surviving. A sign over the gate leading into a training camp of the Gross Deutschland (Greater Germany) elite division claimed "we are born to die." While this is true for all humans, the young Germans in training were left in no doubt that in their case it would probably be sooner rather than later. Through much of the war, the Russian army attacked with massed waves of infantry, which the Germans cut down in large numbers. When Russians finally managed to reach the Germans in their foxholes or trenches, they were not likely to show any mercy. The biggest and bloodiest battles of World War II were fought in this atmosphere of terror and hatred.

Reichsführer Heinrich Himmler, one of the leading Nazis, responsible for the deaths of millions of people in Russia

In a speech in 1943, Heinrich Himmler, Reichsführer of the SS (*Schutzstaffel*—the Nazi elite corps), made it absolutely clear to a group of SS officers how they were expected to behave on the Eastern front:

"We must be honest, decent, loyal and comradely to members of our own blood and to no one else. Whether the other peoples live in comfort or perish of hunger interests me only so far as we need them as slaves for our culture; apart from that it does not interest me. Whether or not 10,000 Russian women collapse from exhaustion while digging a tank ditch interests me only in so far as the tank ditch is completed for Germany."

Source: Joachim C. Fest: *The Face of the Third Reich*

Stalingrad

In 1942, Hitler decided to concentrate his efforts in the south, as the German army didn't have the strength to attack the entire country. The great victories of 1941 had already cost a million casualties. In the central and northern areas, the fighting turned into static warfare—in some ways resembling the Western front in World War I. In the south, the German Sixth Army fought its way to the city of Stalingrad while other forces headed farther south to the oilfields of the Caucasus.

A Soviet anti-tank unit moving up to Stalingrad. Discipline was strict. Any inclination to doubt the Red Army's ability to win the battle was considered high treason, for which a soldier could be shot on the spot.

Germans tanks advance cautiously into a Russian village during the winter of 1942. The German attempt to break through and rescue the soldiers at Stalingrad failed.

Stalingrad was an industrial city stretching for 25 miles (40 km) along the western bank of the mighty Volga River. The name means "Stalin's City" (it is known today as Volgograd). It had a pre-war population of more than half a million. On August 23, 1942, the *Luftwaffe* bombed the city. Soon, German units forced their way through the outer defenses. The Russians had often pulled back before, but as the Germans moved farther into the city, resistance stiffened. The German tanks and infantry found the street fighting much harder than battle on the open plains. More and more units were thrown into the battle. It cost the Germans thousands of men just to take one tractor factory in the northern part of the city. The Germans expected victory, but Russian units kept on fighting and were reinforced from the east bank of the Volga by risky river crossings at night.

In November, the Soviet general Georgy Konstantinovich Zhukov counter-attacked in a pincer maneuver around Stalingrad. The Germans' lines of communications back to the west were dangerously long and guarded only by weak Romanian divisions. Hitler had been warned about this, but got rid of the generals who told him things he did not like to hear. Now the rear defenses crumbled under the weight of an attack by one million Russian soldiers supported by 13,500 guns and almost 900 tanks. The Russians were not vastly superior in numbers, but they were much better motivated. Soon, the German forces in Stalingrad were surrounded. At first, they might have been able to fight their way out of the encirclement, but Hitler would have none of it. A force trying to fight its way into Stalingrad failed to do so.

The trapped Germans could only watch the flashes of guns fading away as the Russians pressed the relief forces farther and farther west.

Winter in Stalingrad

The German soldiers in Stalingrad now faced a winter of utter terror. Hermann Goering, commander-in-chief of the *Luftwaffe*, promised to supply them by air, but it proved to be a task beyond the air force's capabilities. Staying warm in temperatures far below zero became a battle in itself. Breaking out from Stalingrad became impossible, because there was not enough fuel for the tanks and vehicles. Most of the German army depended on horses rather than trucks for its mobility. On Christmas Eve, the German soldiers feasted on 5 oz. (150 g) of bread, 3 oz. (90 g) of meat, 1 oz. (30 g) of butter and some coffee—a luxury meal by Stalingrad's standards. But as food ran out, the situation worsened and the soldiers ate their horses, though this put to rest any final dreams of escape. There was no help for the wounded or for those who were suffering from frostbite.

Hitler had promised to supply the besieged Germans in Stalingrad by air. It was a task far beyond the capability of the German air force. Lacking sufficient numbers of suitable transport aircraft, the pilot of this Heinkel 111 bomber had been given the task of flying cargo to the city.

On January 24, the German commander asked for permission to surrender as there seemed to be no point in prolonging the suffering of his doomed men. He got this answer from Hitler: "Surrender is forbidden. Sixth Army will hold their positions to the last man and the last round and by their heroic endurance will make an unforgettable contribution toward the establishment of a defensive front and the salvation of the Western world."

A map of Stalingrad showing Russian troops closing in on the German army—making a ring of steel and fire around the city. Inside, the Sixth Army was trapped and heading for disaster.

The Russians could have let the Germans freeze and starve to death. But they attacked, and, in spite of Hitler's orders, the last Germans surrendered on February 2, 1943. Between August 1942 and February 1943, Germany and the Axis powers lost 3,500 tanks, 12,000 guns, 3,000 aircraft, and 1.5 million men—dead, wounded, or captured—on the Eastern front. Of the 330,000 surrounded in Stalingrad, only 91,000 lived long enough to surrender. Many of these survivors were appallingly weak and sick. Marching through the winter to prison camps, more than half of them died within weeks. Only 5,000 made it back to Germany after the war.

Stalingrad was a shock to the Germans. The Soviets had fought well, and by competent maneuvering around the city, they had completely annihilated the German Sixth Army. No setback in the war so far came anywhere near this total disaster for the Germans.

| 0 | | 50 | | 100 km |
| 0 | | | 50 miles | |

U S S R

R. Volga

Kalach

Stalingrad

Sixth Army
(General Paulus)
and Fourth Army
(General Hoth)

N

Logovsky

Kotelnikovo

R. Don

Key

→ **Russian advances**

— **Front line 2 Nov 1942**

--- **Front line 30 Nov 1942**

A German lieutenant of a panzer division wrote:

"We have fought during fifteen days for a single house, with mortars, grenades, machine-guns and bayonets. Already, by the third day, 54 German corpses are strewn in the cellars, on the landings and in the staircases. The front is a corridor between burnt-out rooms; it is the thin ceiling between two floors. Help comes from neighbouring houses by fire escapes and chimneys. There is a ceaseless struggle from noon to night. From storey to storey, faces black with sweat, we bombard each other with grenades in the middle of explosions, clouds of dust and smoke, heaps of mortar, floods of blood, fragments of furniture and human beings. Ask any soldier what half an hour of hand-to-hand struggle means in such a fight. And imagine Stalingrad; 80 days and 80 nights of hand-to-hand struggles."

Source: Alan Clark: *Barbarossa*

A female fighter-pilot

Traditionally, women have not often taken part in battle, but it shows just how intensively the Russians mobilized its resources that some women were allowed to serve in combat units. One of the best known—fighter-pilot Lilya Litvyak—fought at Stalingrad. Initially, like other female pilots, she had difficulty in being accepted by her male colleagues, but she proved her ability by flying over Stalingrad and shooting down German planes. In 1943, she downed a high-scoring German fighter pilot. He survived the crash and was confronted by his victor. He thought it was all a joke, until Lilya described in great detail how she had outflown him and shot him down. Lilya Litvyak was killed in action on August 1, 1943. Her body was found only many years later. In 1990, she was posthumously awarded the highest military order "Hero of the Soviet Union" by Mikhail Gorbachev.

Source: Bruce Myles: *Night Witches*/Hugh Morgan: *Soviet Aces of WW2*

Lilya Litvyak— Soviet fighter-pilot

Russian partisans sabotaging a train line leading to the Kursk area in 1943

Kursk

On July 5, 1943, the Germans launched an offensive in Kursk, a city between Stalingrad and Moscow. The German army had managed to assemble strong forces for the offensive. This had not been without difficulty because partisans in the German-occupied areas of Russia had blown up hundreds of supply trains. In the Mediterranean, 250,000 Germans had recently surrendered in Africa, and combined U.S. and British forces now threatened Italy. This front would need soldiers and weapons, too. It was, nonetheless, an impressive force that went into the attack, hoping to do what it had done several times before in Russia—surround, capture, or kill enemy soldiers in large numbers. Hitler told his soldiers that victory in Kursk would be a "shining beacon for the whole world." But the Russians expected the attack and had prepared strong defensive positions.

At first, the Germans advanced but their offensive quickly ran out of steam. Their new types of tanks were difficult to knock out, but the Russians found the weak spots and overwhelmed them with large numbers of their own tanks. Kursk turned out to be the biggest tank battle in history. On July 12, 850 Russian tanks fought in close combat with nearly 700 German tanks. Official Soviet history has described how "The battlefield seemed too small for the hundreds of armored machines...The detonation of the guns merged into a continuous menacing howl...Shells fired at short range penetrated both front and side armor of the tanks. While this was going on there were frequent explosions as ammunition blew up, while tank turrets, blown off by the explosions, were thrown dozens of meters away from the twisted machines."

Russian tanks had simple designs but heavy armor and weapons—they were more than a match for the German tanks and stronger than the tanks of the Western Allies. These T34s are heading for Kursk.

Retreat

The German offensive in Kursk failed dismally, and soon the Germans were being pushed back. From July to October 1943, German losses totaled 907,000 men. The Russians suffered too, but were able to replace their fighting troops. Already in 1942, the Soviets had produced 24,400 tanks against the German's 4,800. Thus the Soviet army grew stronger while the German was never again able to launch an offensive in the east. For the Germans, the Eastern front became a desperate struggle to stop the advancing Russians. A posting to the Eastern front almost equaled a death sentence to a German soldier. Two years after Hitler had attacked Russia, the back of his army had been broken by the nation he had expected to knock out with a single hard blow.

Line-up for the Battle of Kursk

	German	Russian
Soldiers	900,000	1,337,000
Artillery	10,000	20,220
Tanks	2,700	3,306
Aircraft	2,500	2,650

Source: Geoffrey Jukes: *Kursk*

Defeated German soldiers marching into Soviet captivity. Few of the men would ever see Germany again.

Bomber offensive

The longest battle of World War II was fought in the skies over Germany. Bombers of the Royal Air Force (RAF), and later also the U.S. Army Air Force (USAAF) took the war to every corner of Germany in a campaign that lasted almost from the first to the last day of the war. Some imagined that the bombing would be the decisive factor in winning the war.

Strategic bombing

After World War I, some claimed that future wars could be won by bomber aircraft alone. The bombers would always somehow get through to their targets. If these targets were weapon factories, oil refineries, harbors, and railroads then the enemy would lose the war because they would have no weapons, fuel, or means of transportation. The theory also suggested that the civilian population of the enemy could be the target. Then panic would break out, and the shocked civilians would force their government to surrender. The officers responsible for the strategy of the RAF and the USAAF believed this theory to be correct. Whereas the air forces of Germany and Russia were trained to fight directly alongside soldiers and tanks at the front, the main purpose of the RAF and the USAAF was to be strategic bombing—which meant attacking the factories and towns of their enemies.

The seven-man crew of a British four-engined Halifax bomber studies the map before takeoff.

Early in World War II, both RAF Bomber Command and the *Luftwaffe* discovered that some bombers would get through defenses, but far from all of them. In fact, without a fighter escort, some bomber squadrons were wiped out completely. No fighter escorts had the range to follow the bombers to distant targets. Bombers began to fly at night. In the darkness, it was difficult for the fighters to intercept them. It was also difficult for the

Preparing 1,000 lb (453 kg) bombs for a Lancaster in 1942. The British heavy bombers carried by far the heaviest bomb loads in the European theater of war.

bombers to find their target. During the early war years, British bombers had to navigate using only a map, watch, and compass. Over a completely blacked-out Germany, this was far from easy. It was assumed that the bombers could hit targets like oil refineries and railroad yards—and occasionally they did so. But a survey carried out in 1941 concluded that only 20 percent of the bombers got within 5 miles (8 km) of their target—in other words, the average bomber crew was not able to find its target at all.

Area bombing

In 1942, RAF Bomber Command changed its policy. Bomber squadrons were equipped with heavier, four-engined bombers. Scientists worked hard to develop navigational aids, and a pathfinder force was created to help the bombers find their way at night. It was also decided that the smallest target the bombers could be expected to hit was a town. From February 1942, the RAF started area bombing the neighborhoods of German industrial workers. In a letter to RAF Bomber Command it was pointed out that "the aiming points are to be the built-up areas, not, for instance, the dockyards or aircraft factories...this must be made quite clear if it is not understood."

From 1943, RAF Bomber Command had the means to hit Germany hard. During the early months, the industrial cities of the Ruhr were targeted. In the summer, Hamburg was bombed, and during the winter Berlin and other cities were hit. These three periods have become known as the battle of the Ruhr, the battle of Hamburg, and the battle of Berlin. A raid would involve perhaps 700 bombers—mostly four-engined types. The first wave of aircraft would drop heavy bombs to blow in roofs and windows. The second wave would drop thousands of small incendiary bombs,

creating large number of fires. Finally, a last wave would drop more incendiaries to sustain the fires, and ordinary bombs to prevent the fire brigades putting them out. City after city in Germany burned despite the German's efforts to stop the bombing. Some bombings, such as Hamburg in 1943 and Dresden in 1945, are remembered for the large number of German civilians killed. These attacks were not planned any differently from hundreds of others: they just succeeded far beyond expectation. The result for German civilians and their towns was complete devastation.

A night flight carried out by airmen from a British airfield would mostly be uneventful. But out of the darkness, the shadow of a night fighter might appear. Seconds of quick reaction, accurate shooting, or evasive

"Dambusting" Lancasters of 617 Squadron RAF destroyed the Möhne and Eder dams in the German Ruhr district in May 1943. It was a successful attempt to stop German industry by denying it essential electricity and water.

41

The air war against Germany was launched from Great Britain. The range of fighter cover increased during the war. By 1943, the Mustang escorts could fly escort missions deep into Germany and continued to do so until the Luftwaffe was finally defeated.

action would then decide if the bomber survived. Once it reached its target, the bomber had to fly straight for some time to aim the bombs, which made the plane very vulnerable. Some hours later, the crew would be back to see the dawn break over the peaceful English countryside—if they made it back at all. From the numbers of aircraft missing after raids, it was clear that the chances of surviving were poor. In fact, on average, the German civilians being bombed stood a much better chance of survival than the young men bombing them.

An airman flying bombers with the RAF had to fly a "tour" of 30 operations. These figures show what on average happened to 100 men in RAF Bomber Command.

Killed on operations	51
Killed in crashes in England	9
Seriously injured in crashes	3
Prisoners of war (some injured)	12
Shot down but evaded capture	1
Survived unharmed	24

Source: Middlebrook: *The Nuremberg Raid*

Over the target

Don Charlwood, an Australian navigator flying Lancasters with RAF Bomber Command, described the harrowing, dangerous moments over the target:

"I would try to tell myself then that this was a city, a place inhabited by beings such as ourselves, a place with the familiar sights of civilization. But the thought would carry only little conviction. A German city was always this, this hellish picture of flame, gunfire and searchlights, an unreal picture because we could not hear it or feel its breath. Sometimes, when the smoke rolled back and we saw streets and buildings, I felt startled. Perhaps if we had seen white upturned faces of people, as over England we sometimes did, our hearts would have rebelled..."

Source: Charlwood: *No Moon Tonight*

Enter the Eighth Air Force

In 1943, the U.S. Eighth Air Force had built up large forces in England. Flying from England, it would join RAF Bomber Command in the air offensive against Germany. The Americans planned to bomb key industries rather than burn down residential areas. This required precision bombing in daylight.

A Lancaster bomber outlined against a background of fire and flak over Hamburg, August 1943. The city was devastated in just over a week.

When U.S. Boeing B-17 Flying Fortresses were escorted by Mustang fighters, they could reach far into Germany.

The Americans assumed that British and German bombers had not been able to survive daylight operations because they had not been heavily armed. The U.S. Flying Fortresses and Liberators were each equipped with about ten machine guns. Flying in large formations, it was believed that they could support each other and meet the German fighters with a wall of fire.

In 1943, the U.S. bombers began flying missions deep into Germany. They could only be escorted part of the way by fighters that did not have enough fuel to fly into Germany. So the Germans were able to attack U.S. bombers once the fighters had turned to go home and, in spite of their heavy machine guns, the U.S. bombers were unable to protect themselves against this onslaught. For a while, flights deep into Germany had to be stopped. The U.S. answer to the problem was a crash program to build Mustang fighters. This aircraft had not been a great success at first, but when fitted with a Rolls-Royce engine it became one of the best fighters of the war. Most important, it was able to fly to Berlin and back. Protected by Mustangs, the U.S. bombers flew all over Germany in 1944. In air battles that were bigger than any other seen before or since, the *Luftwaffe* was defeated.

Whereas the U.S. formations grew larger and the crews increasingly more experienced, it was very difficult for the Germans to replace lost crews with anything but young, partly trained pilots. By the summer of 1944, most German fighter pilots had only between 8 and 30 hours' combat experience. By then, U.S. attacks on fuel-producing plants made it difficult for the Germans to use fuel at all for flying training. If the back of the German army was broken on the Eastern front, then the back of the *Luftwaffe* was broken by the USAAF in the big air battles over Germany. The superiority gained in the air was vital for the successful landing of Allied forces in Normandy.

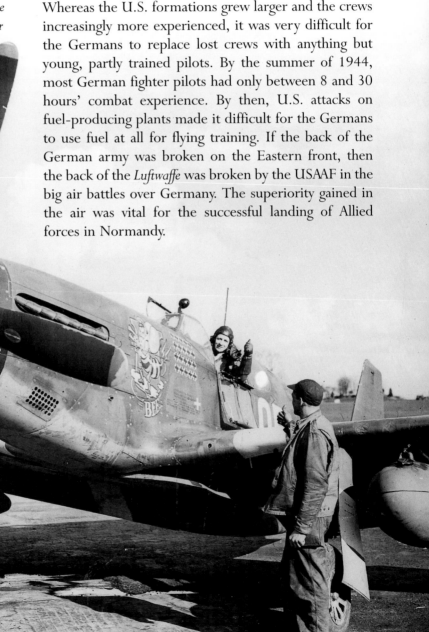

A Mustang about to take off for an escort mission—note the long-range fuel tanks under the wings.

The second front

The bombers did not win the war on their own, as some officers had hoped. German morale did not break down, and, during 1943–44, the Germans actually increased their arms production in spite of the bombings. But the relentless bombing also put a mental strain on the Germans soldiers at the front in knowing that their families were not safe back home. Albert Speer, responsible for German arms production, has described how the defensive measures were very expensive for Germany: "The barrels of ten thousand anti-aircraft guns were pointing towards the sky. The same guns could well have been employed in Russia against tanks. Had it not been for the air front over Germany, our defensive strength against tanks would have been about doubled. Moreover, the anti-aircraft force tied down hundreds of thousands of young

Hamburg in ruins in 1945. These houses have been destroyed largely by British fire bomb attacks, as most of the walls are still standing. Everything inside has been burned out. When people sheltered in the cellars underneath such houses, many died from the heat or lack of oxygen.

soldiers. A third of our optical industry was busy producing gunsights for the flak batteries. About half of our electronics industry was engaged in producing radar and communications networks for defense against bombing. Simply because of this, the supply of our frontline troops with modern equipment remained far behind that of the Western armies."

During the years 1942–43, the Soviet Union was desperately fighting to throw out the German invaders. Millions of Soviet soldiers and civilians were killed. Stalin wanted Great Britain and the United States to open a second front in Western Europe. The Western Allies preferred to wait until Germany had been weakened before landing soldiers in Europe. Until then, the second front consisted of the bomber offensive. It was one of many costly battles of attrition that, in the end, forced Germany to its knees.

The big raids on Germany continue. British war plants share with the R.A.F. credit for these giant operations.

THE ATTACK BEGINS IN THE FACTORY

A British poster urging factory workers to produce more bombs for the attacks on German cities

Losses

During the hard air battles during January to June 1944, the USAAF carried out a survey to study its losses of heavy bombers during 25 missions—the number a U.S. airman was required to fly. On mission one, 2,051 airmen took off with the bombers. On each of the 25 missions, men were lost in action—the worst loss being 139 men and the lightest loss being three.

After mission 25, only 559 (27 percent) of the men survived unharmed. In one important respect a U.S. pilot was luckier than his RAF counterpart. If his Flying Fortress was hit, he stood a much better chance of escaping from the aircraft and parachuting down to the ground than the British airman did.

Remembering

Combat flying put enormous strain on the airmen. On August 17, 1943, Lieutenant Leo Lacasse of the U.S. Eighth Air Force flew from Great Ashfield in Suffolk on a costly mission to bomb an aircraft factory in Regensburg:

"Our losses were heavy. By the time of the Regensburg mission, I had been in combat several times in 60 days and already I was a seasoned war veteran. I had turned 23 and matured far beyond my age... The memories never go away. I have visited my old airfield a number of times since. The silence is always deafening, and the tears are uncontrollable."

Source: Middlebrook: *The Schweinfurt-Regensburg Mission*

U.S. Army Air Force Marauder *bombers on a mission to carry out raids on streets and railroads behind German lines in France, 1944.*

The Battle of the Atlantic

Even before the attack on Pearl Harbor in 1941, American servicemen were fighting and dying in the Atlantic. Although neutral, the United States did not want Great Britain to lose the war, and, during the early months of 1941, a British defeat became a distinct possibility. Great Britain was dependent on imports of food, fuel, and raw materials from merchant ships. These ships were being sunk in increasing numbers by German U-boats. Churchill admitted that "the only thing that ever really frightened me during the war was the U-boat peril."

The Royal Navy had prepared for a war against large surface ships. So had the U.S. Navy, not least in the Pacific, assuming that Great Britain would rule the Atlantic waves. When war came, both navies were short of small ships for escort duties. Fortunately, the German navy had not realized just how effective its U-boats would be, so it too had used many resources building

A painting of an Atlantic battle as seen from the deck of a British destroyer. Despite the danger of the U-boat, in the early years of the war, many British ships avoided destruction because of defective German torpedoes.

heavy cruisers and battleships. As it turned out, the large ships never seriously slowed down the flow of goods into Great Britain. The Royal Navy kept a careful watch on them and the mighty German battleship, the *Bismarck*, was hunted down and sunk in a dramatic sea battle. But the most important Atlantic battles were fought between U-boats and the small escort ships.

Convoys

During World War I, it was realized that merchant ships suffered fewer losses if they sailed in convoy. So in World War II, Great Britain introduced the convoy system as soon as the war started. Ships in convoy sailed in groups protected by navy ships. Naturally, the slowest ship in the convoy dictated the speed of the rest. Ships had to wait for each other before they could set out on their journey, and there was congestion in harbors as many ships arrived at the same time. Ships in a convoy were less efficient than ships sailing on their own. Great Britain's imports were immediately cut by one third because of this system.

An Atlantic convoy heading for Great Britain in 1943—note how effectively an aircraft may keep watch over a large expanse of ocean around the ships.

At first, neither navy ships nor aircraft could provide escort all the way across the Atlantic. The U-boats therefore attacked in the mid-Atlantic. For this reason, the U.S. Navy took responsibility for some of the escort duties in the western Atlantic in 1941. The United States effectively joined the war before any official declaration of war was made. Yet escort ships were still in short supply. Even in 1943, a convoy of forty ships might be escorted by only five corvettes—small escort ships that struggled to provide cover.

A view from the conning-tower of a U-boat. German U-boats cruised on the surface because they moved very slowly when they were submerged.

U-boats kept in radio contact and attacked in "wolf packs". To do this, the U-boats had to be on the surface, during the day. At night, they attacked on the surface too—a U-boat was almost impossible to see in the dark. Submerging was only used as a means of escaping. Once the U-boats had found a convoy, they caused immense destruction.

However, in the convoy battles of 1943, the German U-boats began to suffer such heavy losses that they no longer represented a great threat. They were defeated by technology. Radar made it possible for aircraft and escort ships to find them in the dark, even though they could not be seen with the naked eye. From 1943, the long-range aircraft covering the mid-Atlantic could force several U-boats to submerge, making it impossible for them to find and attack convoys. Considering how many bombers were used for the attacks on Germany, it is surprising that long-range aircraft were not provided earlier for the protection of convoys.

Casualties

U.S. Captain John Waters, who took part in the convoy battles of World War II, made the point that the number of deaths in the Battle of the Atlantic was greater than the total number of deaths in all naval battles of the previous 500 years. Of the 40,900 Germans sailing in the U-boats, 63 percent were killed, and 12 percent were captured. The sailors on the merchant ships suffered much higher casualty rates than many units in the military services.

Wartime sailing put an enormous strain on the sailors. Those who survived were often troubled by the memories long after the war. Nobody who sailed in the convoys ever forgot the screams of men floating in the burning oil of a sinking tanker or the cries for help from men hoping to be found and picked up from their life rafts in the dark and icy north Atlantic.

U-boat crewmen stood little chance of surviving if their boats were hit. This U-boat crew has been lucky and has been taken aboard a British destroyer.

A sub-lieutenant described how his escort ship was engaged in rescuing survivors from a convoy on a stormy night in 1943:

"The American captain was in a lifeboat with a black steward who was in a very bad way, mainly from exposure and swallowing oil. The boat was on the weatherside of the ship and one moment level with the rail, the next thirty feet [9 m] below us. We managed to grab the captain eventually when the boat was on the upsurge, but couldn't get the steward. We steamed in a circle, not easy in the weather we were having, and got the boat on our lee side. We got the man in, but he died shortly afterwards."

Source: Middlebrook: *Convoy*

Merchant seamen lost in the Atlantic

A job in the merchant navy was a civil occupation, but it was so dangerous that young men in Great Britain could volunteer for it rather than join the military services. The casualty figures illustrate how there was a united effort of many nations to sail essential cargo across the Atlantic in World War II.

United Kingdom	22,490
India (in UK ships)	6,093
China (in UK ships)	2,023
United States	5,662
Norway	4,675
Greece	2,000
Holland (Netherlands)	1,914
Denmark	1,886
Canada	1,437
Belgium	893
South Africa	182
Australia	109
New Zealand	72

Source: Middlebrook: *Convoy*

Fortunate survivors being rescued during the Battle of the Atlantic

Normandy to the German border

On June 6, 1944, Allied forces landed on the French beaches of Normandy in the largest amphibious operation in history. Years of building up forces in England and months of careful preparations were over. Paratroopers had already landed in Normandy under cover of darkness. All over Europe, people under German occupation had waited for this day—D-Day.

Right: A map of the Normandy landings and the drive to the German border. British and Canadian forces landed on Sword, Juno, and Gold beaches. U.S. troops landed on Utah and Omaha beaches.

Thousands of ships sailed the soldiers to five beaches code-named Utah, Omaha, Gold, Juno, and Sword. At the end of D-Day, 132,000 American, British, and Canadian troops had landed. In some places they had met little opposition. There had been severe fighting on Omaha, with American soldiers being pinned down on the beach and suffering heavy casualties. But thanks to superior firepower, air support, and great courage from officers and men on the beach, the Americans fought through at Omaha, too. During the weeks that followed, more and more men and supplies were unloaded on the beaches. By August, two million Allied and German soldiers were fighting in Normandy. The Allied armies needed over 26,000 tons of supplies (food and ammunition) each day. Allied air superiority made it difficult for the Germans to get their supplies to the battlefield.

Above: Landing at Omaha beach, Normandy. After the Germans had been pushed back from the beach, thousands of men, tanks, vehicles, and vast amounts of supplies were then taken ashore.

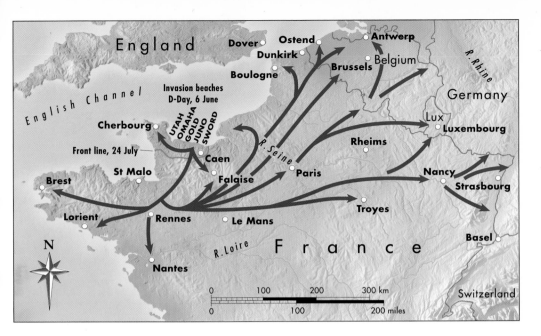

Battle for Normandy

The landing had been a success, but Normandy proved to be a difficult place in which to fight. The landscape was dominated by tall hedges and small fields. There were places everywhere for soldiers and tanks to hide. Casualties mounted as the battle raged from hedgerow to hedgerow, from village to village. The Germans skillfully made many small counterattacks, which were often very dangerous operations. Many of the Germans knew that this would be their last chance to stop the Allies. Their last battles were enforced by the strict German discipline and Hitler's refusal to give way to the Allies.

Eventually, the German army was trapped in a pocket near Falaise. Some soldiers surrendered, some escaped, but many were killed in a ghastly slaughter by artillery and rocket-firing fighters. Altogether, Germany lost 450,000 men in Normandy—210,000 taken as prisoners of war. The victory had cost the

They had to do it

On D-Day, Jim Fudge was manning a gun on a U.S. Navy landing ship sailing for Omaha beach:

"We had army engineers aboard. These were fellows who had already made the Sicily and Italian invasions. They were frightened. We weren't battle-seasoned, but these fellows were. They weren't happy about going into D-Day. They just wanted to come out alive. Once you've been through something like this, you realize how dangerous it is. People really do get killed out there. They wanted no part of it, but of course they had to do it. They didn't have the wide-eyed patriotic gung-ho 'let's go get 'em, fellows' attitude. Theirs was a bit more cynical."

Source: *Interview with the author*

German prisoners after the slaughter at Falaise. Surrendering to the Western Allies at this stage of the war meant that these prisoners stood a good chance of returning home after the war was over.

Falaise killing ground

RAF pilot Desmond Scott visited the Falaise battleground after the Germans had surrendered:

"*The roads were choked with the wreckage and the swollen bodies of men and horses. Bits of uniform were plastered to shattered tanks and trucks and human remains hung in grotesque shapes on the blackened hedgerows. Corpses lay in pools of dried blood, staring into space and as if their eyes were being forced from their sockets. Two grey-clad bodies, both minus their legs, leaned against a clay bank as if in prayer. I picked up a photograph of a smiling young German recruit standing between his parents, two solemn peasants who stared back at me in accusation...*"

Source: Hastings: *Overlord*

Allies 206,672 casualties—36,976 men were killed. At the end of August there was almost nothing to stop the Allies from advancing, although they had to wait for their supplies to keep up with them. In September, a British attempt to secure the bridges over the Rhine failed at Arnhem. The Germans were able to establish defensive lines in the west—and the war continued.

Battle of the Bulge

On December 16, 1944, the Germans launched an offensive in the Ardennes. They had skillfully concealed the build-up for the offensive and the extent of it came as a surprise to the Allies. In order to deny the Allies the use of their superior air forces, the attack was made on a foggy day with bad weather forecasts for the following days. The Germans advanced quickly, creating the "bulge" in the front lines. The American units held out in the town of Bastogne. At first, the Germans decided to bypass them, only to find out that they needed to control Bastogne because it was an important five-road network. Fierce fighting resulted, but the Americans refused to give up. When they realized just how heavy the German attack was, Allied ground forces were hurried to the Ardennes front. General George S. Patton performed the impossible, disengaging his Third Army from western Germany, and turning 90 degrees. In just two days Patton moved 133,000 vehicles and men 75 miles (120 km) to the north to push the Germans back.

U.S. artillery in action during the Battle of the Bulge

When the skies cleared, just over a week after the offensive began, thousands of planes hit the German positions, columns on the roads, railroads, and communications centers on December 23. Soon, the Germans were running short of fuel, food, and ammunition. Around Bastogne, tracks of German tanks in the snow exposed their hidden positions under the trees. Napalm, rockets, and bombs set the area on fire. Many soldiers had hoped the war would be over by Christmas— fighting hard, the men realized that many would never make it back home. The "bulge" was cleared by late January 1945. The fighting had cost the Allies 77,000 casualties and the Germans at least 110,000. Though the fighting was as hard as any, the outcome of the battle was never seriously in doubt. Germany had used up its last reserves in the west. The Allies could replace their losses of weapons and equipment within weeks.

Fighting to the very end

The Battle of the Bulge was Nazi Germany's last great attempt to stop the advancing U.S. and British armies. Hitler had dreamed of a new turning point, but he lost that final large-scale offensive. Smaller-scale battles were still being fought by the U.S. and British armies in different parts of the world. To the very end, soldiers experienced the harrowing sights and sounds of battle—heads, arms, and legs being blown off by exploding mines and artillery shells, men trapped in burning tanks, and soldiers breaking down under the tremendous pressures of combat.

An American pilot poses in front of his Thunderbolt fighter-bomber. Endless attacks by Allied aircraft put to rest any German hopes that the Battle of the Bulge might be a new turning point in the war.

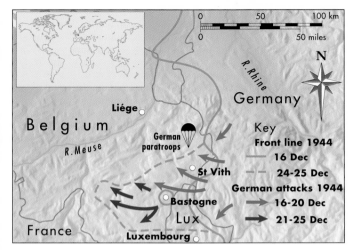

This map shows the German offensive in the Ardennes. Lightly armored U.S. divisions were trapped at Bastogne, surrounded by a German infantry division and two panzer divisions.

It is difficult to see the sense for Germany in fighting its last battles—the Battle of the Bulge included. They caused much suffering, more casualties, and yet they only delayed the inevitable defeat of Germany. The final outcome for Germany would eventually be a disarmed and divided nation, deprived of its power to make war, and losing territory to Poland and Russia. By early May 1945, the war was over in Europe.

For you the war is over

During the Battle of the Bulge, aircraft effectively stopped all German movement in daylight—but did so at great risk. An American pilot recalls his experiences:

"We dropped our napalm bombs on them and went down to strafe. Anti-aircraft opened up on us and we had to break formation. I located the gun emplacement and dived down to strafe its location, but did not see another gun to my side. It made several hits. My engine quit and a fire started near my right foot in the cockpit. I flipped open the canopy, unfastened the seatbelt, stood up and dived for the trailing edge of the wing. My leg hit the tail of the plane, my chute opened. I swung once and hit the ground, rolling into the anti-aircraft position I had been strafing seconds before. The German gunner very carefully removed my 45 automatic, and with his knife cut the chute cords from around me and said 'for you the var ist over!'"

Source: Parker: Adapted from *To Win the Winter Sky*

Date list

<table>
<tr><td colspan="2"><u>1937</u></td></tr>
<tr><td>July 7</td><td>Japan invades China.</td></tr>
<tr><td colspan="2"><u>1939</u></td></tr>
<tr><td>Sept. 1</td><td>Germany invades Poland.</td></tr>
<tr><td>Sept. 3</td><td>France and Great Britain declare war on Germany.</td></tr>
<tr><td colspan="2"><u>1940</u></td></tr>
<tr><td>April 9</td><td>Germany invades Denmark and Norway.</td></tr>
<tr><td>May 10</td><td>Germany invades France, Belgium, Luxembourg, and the Netherlands.</td></tr>
<tr><td>June 22</td><td>France surrenders to Germany. Great Britain stands alone.</td></tr>
<tr><td>July 10</td><td>Battle of Britain begins —first major battle in world history fought entirely in the air.</td></tr>
<tr><td>Sept. 13</td><td>Italian forces invade Egypt.</td></tr>
<tr><td>Sept. 17</td><td>German plans to invade England are postponed.</td></tr>
<tr><td>Dec. 9</td><td>British offensive in Egypt pushes the Italians back.</td></tr>
<tr><td colspan="2"><u>1941</u></td></tr>
<tr><td>Feb. 12</td><td>Rommel arrives in Tripoli, North Africa.</td></tr>
<tr><td>April</td><td>Record number of sinkings by German U-boats.</td></tr>
<tr><td>April 6</td><td>German forces invade Greece and Yugoslavia.</td></tr>
<tr><td>April 17</td><td>Yugoslavia surrenders to Germany.</td></tr>
<tr><td>April 27</td><td>Greece surrenders to Germany.</td></tr>
<tr><td>May 27</td><td>The German battleship, the Bismarck, is sunk.</td></tr>
<tr><td>June 22</td><td>The German attack on the Soviet Union begins— Operation Barbarossa.</td></tr>
</table>

<table>
<tr><td>Aug. 20</td><td>German forces close in on Leningrad. The siege lasts 890 days and 830,000 Russians in the city die.</td></tr>
<tr><td>Oct. 2</td><td>German attack on Moscow.</td></tr>
<tr><td>Dec. 6</td><td>Russian counteroffensive saves Moscow.</td></tr>
<tr><td>Dec. 7</td><td>Japan attacks U.S. base at Pearl Harbor, Hawaii.</td></tr>
<tr><td>Dec. 8</td><td>U.S. and Great Britain declare war on Japan.</td></tr>
<tr><td>Dec. 11</td><td>Hitler declares war on the United States.</td></tr>
<tr><td>Oct. 17</td><td>First U.S. destroyer torpedoed.</td></tr>
<tr><td>Dec. 25</td><td>Hong Kong falls to Japan.</td></tr>
<tr><td>Dec. 31</td><td>U.S. warship torpedoed.</td></tr>
<tr><td colspan="2"><u>1942</u></td></tr>
<tr><td>Jan. 7</td><td>Sarawak captured by Japan.</td></tr>
<tr><td>Jan. 12</td><td>Kuala Lumpur in Malaya falls to Japan.</td></tr>
<tr><td>Jan. 15</td><td>Invasion of Burma begins.</td></tr>
<tr><td>Jan. 15</td><td>Singapore falls to Japan.</td></tr>
<tr><td>Feb. 19</td><td>Darwin, Australia, bombed.</td></tr>
<tr><td>May 4</td><td>Battle of the Coral Sea begins.</td></tr>
<tr><td>June 4</td><td>Battle of Midway begins.</td></tr>
<tr><td>June 9</td><td>The Japanese conquest of the Philippines is complete.</td></tr>
<tr><td>June 21</td><td>Rommel captures Tobruk, North Africa.</td></tr>
<tr><td>July– Nov.</td><td>Battles of El Alamein fought in the desert.</td></tr>
<tr><td>Aug. 7</td><td>U.S. Marines land at Guadalcanal.</td></tr>
<tr><td>Aug. 12</td><td>Montgomery takes command of the British Army in North Africa.</td></tr>
<tr><td>Aug. 25</td><td>Battle of Stalingrad begins.</td></tr>
<tr><td>Nov. 1</td><td>Montgomery breaks through at El Alamein.</td></tr>
<tr><td>Nov. 8</td><td>Operation Torch: Allied invasion of North Africa.</td></tr>
</table>

Nov. 19	Russian counterattack at Stalingrad. The German Sixth Army is surrounded in the city.	June 27	U.S. troops capture Cherbourg.
		July 9	British and Canadian troops capture Caen.
1943		Aug. 20	German forces are surrounded at Falaise in Normandy.
Jan. 31	First German forces surrender at Stalingrad.		
Feb. 9	Battle for Guadalcanal is over.	Sept. 17	British forces launch unsuccessful paratroop attack on Arnhem, in the Netherlands.
Feb. 14	German forces attack Allied forces at Kasserine Pass in North Africa.		
		Oct. 20	U.S. troops land in the Philippines.
March 5– July 14	The Battle of the Ruhr; British air raids on German industry.	Dec. 16–27	Battle of the Bulge—the last German offensive in the West.
May 13	German and Italian troops surrender in North Africa.	**1945**	
		Feb. 13–14	Allied bombing raid destroys Dresden.
July 5–12	Battle of Kursk—the greatest tank battle in history.	Feb. 23	Stars and Stripes are raised at Iwo Jima.
July 10	Allied landing in Sicily.	March 24	Allies cross the Rhine.
July 24	Allied bombing of Hamburg—air raids cause great destruction.	April 22	Russia launches final nine-day assault against Berlin.
		April 30	Berlin falls to the Russians.
Aug. 17	U.S. deep-penetration daylight raids on Schweinfurt and Regensburg.	April 30	Hitler commits suicide.
		May 7	Germany surrenders.
		May 8	VE (Victory in Europe) Day.
Aug.–March	Bombing of Berlin by air.		
Nov. 5	New offensives by U.S. troops begin in the Solomons.	May 23	Himmler commits suicide.
		June 21	Okinawa finally taken by U.S. troops.
1944			
Jan. 22	Allies land at Anzio, Italy.	Aug. 6	Atomic bomb dropped on Hiroshima, Japan.
Jan. 31	U.S. attack Marshall Islands.		
Feb.–May	Battle of Monte Cassino in Italy.	Aug. 9	Atomic bomb dropped on Nagasaki, Japan.
Feb.–June	German air force suffers severe losses against U.S. long-range fighters.	Aug. 14	Japan surrenders unconditionally to the Allies.
June 6	D-Day landings in Normandy.	Aug. 15	VJ (Victory over Japan) Day.
June 17	Saipan, in the Marianas taken by U.S. troops.	Sept. 2	Japan formally surrenders.

Glossary

aircraft carrier a large ship with a deck where aircraft may take off and land.

amphibious assault an attack from the sea where forces are sailed to the shore.

area bombing a type of bombing attack in which parts of a city are showered with explosives and incendiary bombs.

battleship a large surface ship armed with heavy guns, but less deadly than U-boats and aircraft carriers.

destroyer a medium-sized ship, very maneuverable, armed with guns and torpedoes (explosives).

dive-bomber a bomber aircraft designed to drop its bombs in a steep dive.

dogfight close combat between fighter aircraft.

flak anti-aircraft fire.

foxhole a hole dug in the ground and used by a soldier for protection in battle.

Hurricane the plane that shot down most German aircraft during the Battle of Britain.

incendiary bomb a fire bomb designed to start fires—often small and weighing only a few ounces.

lines of communications the means by which supplies are brought to troops. Long lines make it easier for the enemy to attack the ships and trucks that are carrying the supplies.

malaria a disease carried by female mosquitoes, often found in hot climates. Many U.S. Marines suffered from malaria in the Pacific. In swampy areas of Russia, soldiers also suffered from the disease.

minefield an area where mines have been dug into the ground to stop an advancing enemy.

mobile forces soldiers who are transported over long distances.

napalm a gasoline jelly used as an incendiary in bombs and dropped from aircraft.

panzer armored; usually referring to German armored tank divisions.

paratroopers soldiers transported by plane to drop behind enemy lines by parachute.

partisan a civilian operating as a soldier behind the enemy lines.

RAF (Royal Air Force) the British Air Force.

RAF Bomber Command the British bomber forces during the war.

RAF Fighter Command the British fighter forces during the war.

Spitfire the most important British fighter plane of the war.

strafe a fast air attack with bombs, machine-gun fire, or rockets.

strategic bombing bombing aimed at destroying an enemy's means of fighting—such as factories or transportation systems.

Suez Canal a waterway linking the Mediterranean and the Red Sea.

torpedo bomber an aircraft used to drop torpedoes on ships.

trench a long hole dug in the ground to offer soldiers protection from enemy fire.

U-boats the German submarine fleet.

USAAF (U.S. Army Air Force) most U.S. aircraft were controlled by the army. After the war, the USAAF became known as the U.S. Air Force.

wolf packs groups of German U-boats which together attacked Allied shipping.

Sources and Resources

Further reading

Nicola Barber: *World War II*, Evans Brothers, 1994. A calendar of events of the war and how they affected people all over Europe.

Heneghan, James: *Wish Me Luck. Torpedoed! A World War II Survival Story.* Fictional story of Jamie, an evacuee, aboard a ship bound for Canada. When the ship is torpedoed, Jamie has to fight for his life.

Ken Hills: *World War II—Wars that Changed the World*, Cherrytree Books, 1997. The 'Blitzkrieg' tactics are detailed followed by the details of how the war became global, summarizing important battles, personalities and consequences.

Other sources

Mark Arnold-Foster: *The World at War*, William Collins Sons & Co Ltd, 1973

Martha Byrd: *A World in Flames*, Smithmark Publishers, New York, 1992

Don Charlwood: *No Moon Tonight*, Goodall Publications, London, 1984

Winston Churchill: *World War II*, Cassell & Co. Ltd, London, 1951

Alan Clark: *Barbarossa*, Phoenix, London, 1996

Joachim C. Fest: *The Face of the Third Reich*, Penguin Books, Harmondsworth, England, 1963

Max Hastings: *Bomber Command*, Michael Joseph, London, 1979

Max Hastings: *Overlord*, Pan Books, London, 1985

Geoffrey Jukes: *Kursk*, Ballantine Books, New York, 1972

Geoffrey Jukes: *Stalingrad*, Ballantine Books, New York, 1968

Robert Leckie: *Challenge for the Pacific*, Da Capo Press, 1999

James Lucas: *War on the Eastern Front*, Greenhill Books, London, 1979

Martin Middlebrook: *Convoy*, Allen Lane, London, 1976

Martin Middlebrook: *The Battle of Hamburg*, Allen Lane, London, 1980

Albert Speer: *Inside The Third Reich*, Avon Books, New York, 1971

Dan Van Der Vat: *The Atlantic Campaign*, Grafton, London, 1990

Derek Wood/Derek Dempster: *The Narrow Margin*, Arrow Books, 1969

Internet

There are dozens of websites with information on battles. Just use the name of the battle to start the search. This will lead you to information, museums, memorials, veteran associations, and so on.

Places to visit

Imperial War Museum, London—for general information about the world wars.

Imperial War Museum, Duxford, Cambridgeshire—focuses on the air war, including a special museum on the U.S. engagement in Europe.

HMS Belfast, London—a Second World War cruiser, now a museum of naval warfare.

Many of Second World War battlefields e.g. Normandy in France, have interesting memorials and museums located close by.

Index

If a number is in **bold** type, there is an illustration.